# First World War
## and Army of Occupation
# War Diary
## France, Belgium and Germany

### 57 DIVISION
Headquarters, Branches and Services
Royal Army Ordnance Corps
Deputy Assistant Director Ordnance Services
2 February 1917 - 28 February 1919

WO95/2969/5

The Naval & Military Press Ltd
www.nmarchive.com
Published in association with The National Archives

Published by

## The Naval & Military Press Ltd

Unit 10 Ridgewood Industrial Park,

Uckfield, East Sussex,

TN22 5QE England

Tel: +44 (0) 1825 749494

www.naval-military-press.com

www.nmarchive.com

*This diary has been reprinted in facsimile from the original. Any imperfections are inevitably reproduced and the quality may fall short of modern type and cartographic standards.*

© **Crown Copyright**
**Images reproduced by permission of The National Archives, London, England, 2015.**

# Contents

| Document type | Place/Title | Date From | Date To |
|---|---|---|---|
| Heading | WO95/2969/5 Deputy Assistant Director Ordnance Services | | |
| Heading | 57th Division D.A. Dir Ordnance Serv. Feb 1917-Feb 1919 | | |
| War Diary | Boulogne | 02/02/1917 | 02/02/1917 |
| War Diary | Bailleul | 03/02/1917 | 06/02/1917 |
| War Diary | Merris | 07/02/1917 | 28/02/1917 |
| Heading | War Diary For March | | |
| Heading | On His Majesty's Service. | | |
| War Diary | Bac St Maur | 01/03/1917 | 31/03/1917 |
| Heading | War Diary For Month Of April | | |
| War Diary | Bac St Maur | 01/04/1917 | 30/04/1917 |
| Miscellaneous | D.A.G 3rd Echelon Base | 09/06/1917 | 09/06/1917 |
| War Diary | Bac St Maur | 01/05/1917 | 17/09/1917 |
| War Diary | Norrent Fontes | 18/09/1917 | 18/10/1917 |
| War Diary | Renescure | 19/10/1917 | 19/10/1917 |
| War Diary | Proven | 20/10/1917 | 23/10/1917 |
| War Diary | Elverdinghe | 24/10/1917 | 06/11/1917 |
| War Diary | Zutkerque | 07/11/1917 | 07/12/1917 |
| War Diary | Proven | 08/12/1917 | 08/12/1917 |
| War Diary | Rousbrugge | 09/12/1917 | 17/12/1917 |
| War Diary | F Camp | 18/12/1917 | 31/12/1917 |
| War Diary | International Corner | 01/01/1918 | 02/01/1918 |
| War Diary | Steenwerck | 03/01/1918 | 16/02/1918 |
| War Diary | Merville | 17/02/1918 | 17/03/1918 |
| War Diary | Le Sart | 18/03/1918 | 19/03/1918 |
| War Diary | Doulieu | 20/03/1918 | 24/03/1918 |
| War Diary | Le Montier | 25/03/1918 | 31/03/1918 |
| War Diary | Doulieu | 01/04/1918 | 02/04/1918 |
| War Diary | Merville | 03/04/1918 | 03/04/1918 |
| War Diary | Lucheux | 04/04/1918 | 05/04/1918 |
| War Diary | Coullemont | 06/04/1918 | 09/04/1918 |
| War Diary | Beauquesne | 10/04/1918 | 12/04/1918 |
| War Diary | Lucheux | 13/04/1918 | 13/04/1918 |
| War Diary | Pas en Artois | 14/04/1918 | 05/05/1918 |
| War Diary | Couin | 06/05/1918 | 30/06/1918 |
| War Diary | Authie | 01/07/1918 | 14/07/1918 |
| War Diary | Pas | 15/07/1918 | 28/07/1918 |
| War Diary | Bouquemaison | 29/07/1918 | 29/07/1918 |
| War Diary | Hermaville | 30/07/1918 | 01/08/1918 |
| War Diary | Agnez Lez Duisans | 02/08/1918 | 17/08/1918 |
| War Diary | Berthencourt | 18/08/1918 | 22/08/1918 |
| War Diary | Frevent | 23/08/1918 | 23/08/1918 |
| War Diary | Bavincourt | 24/08/1918 | 29/08/1918 |
| War Diary | Baisy Copse | 30/08/1918 | 07/09/1918 |
| War Diary | Ecoust St Mein | 08/09/1918 | 16/09/1918 |
| War Diary | Bavincourt | 17/09/1918 | 25/09/1918 |
| War Diary | Boyelles | 26/09/1918 | 30/09/1918 |
| War Diary | | 01/10/1918 | 31/10/1918 |
| War Diary | Field | 01/11/1918 | 30/11/1918 |

| War Diary | Petit Ronchin | 01/12/1918 | 03/12/1918 |
| War Diary | Duisans | 04/12/1918 | 28/02/1919 |

WO95/2969/5
Deputy Assistant Director
Ordnance Services

# 57TH DIVISION

## D.A.DIR. ORDNANCE SERV.
## FEB 1917-FEB 1919

**Army Form C. 2118.**

**WAR DIARY**
or
**INTELLIGENCE SUMMARY**
(Erase heading not required.)

D.A.D.O.S
5) #Division

Vol I

Instructions regarding War Diaries and Intelligence Summaries are contained in F.S. Regs., Part II. and the Staff Manual respectively. Title Pages will be prepared in manuscript.

| Place | Date 1916 | Hour | Summary of Events and Information | Remarks and references to Appendices |
|---|---|---|---|---|
| Boulogne | 2 Feb | — | Arrived at Boulogne | |
| Aireland | 3 | — | Proceeded to Bailleul and reported to ADOS II ANZAC Corps. Issued on train 3 days emergency rations + MB clothing. | |
| " | 4 | — | Proceeded with ADOS to Bac St Maur to interview DADOS NZ Division with regard to taking over Offices + duties on arrival of 5) #Division. | |
| " | 5 | — | Returned to base to take over motor lorry, PL stores with clothing etc. Also to complete equipment for med. Dress Winter Brushes. | |
| " | 6 | — | Forwarded to Coy Cadre kit of Unit dependents - attended + corresponded reports in connection with arrival of Unit. | |
| Thiennes | 7 | — | Made arrangements at Messrs for Offices + Ordnance Security. Received blankets, but repairs to truck for Division received blankets, but repairs to truck in Guild, attended at | |
| " | 8 | — | Continued to receive various items in Guild. Per S'Maur r/a tongue re receipt of store. Received Nova + started to issue to Units, marking differences as Units arrived G. Hot respirator blankets attended to personally - going with motor lorries + seeing them at their billets - by this means, the men in many cases been to advantage. 9. Feb. 2 W Blanket + hot respirator at once on arriving at billets - otherwise would have had to wait at cure + merns to draw | |
| " | 9 | | | |
| " | 10 | | | |
| " | 11 | | | |
| " | 12 | | | |
| " | 13 | | | |
| " | 14 | | | |
| " | 15 | | | |

# WAR DIARY
## or
## INTELLIGENCE SUMMARY
*(Erase heading not required.)*

Army Form C. 2118.

LABOS.
By F. Stevenson

| Place | Date | Hour | Summary of Events and Information | Remarks and references to Appendices |
|---|---|---|---|---|
| Merris | 16 | | Made issues to units of F.S. book, Flanders Clothing Sheeting & received stores — Personnel NCOs arrived | |
| | 17 | | " | |
| | 18 | | — | |
| | 19 | | 2nd Lieut Humphreys reported for duty - Proceeded to Pre Le Mesnil to prepare to taking in Nos W2 Or. | |
| | 20 | | " left home to prepare to taking in Nos. 170, 171, 172 & 173 | |
| | 21 | | Machine Gun Companies reported arrival 170, 171, 172 & 173 for duty with Or Proceeded to 2nd NZ Div each taking over. Started Divnl Armourers Shop | |
| | 22 | | Office & workshop from R.3.Or Taking over & receiving stores. | |
| | 23 | | Proceed to Bailleul to purchase items & | |
| | 24 | | Attended Conference NAD Officer Lorry | |
| | 25 | | Went to Hazebrouck for 15 air cylinders | |
| | 26 | | Routine work at Depot | |
| | 27 | | do | |
| | 28 | | do | |

D.A.G.
III rd Echelon

Herewith
War Diary for
March

2/IV/17

B.[signature]
DADOS

DRCS    ON HIS MAJESTY'S SERVICE

Q495/911   D.A.D.OS
Q.985
A971           201   5

B  Orders

# WAR DIARY
## or
## INTELLIGENCE SUMMARY

Army Form C. 2118.

DADOS J-7 Division Vol 2

| Place | Date 1917 | Hour | Summary of Events and Information | Remarks and references to Appendices |
|---|---|---|---|---|
| BAC ST MAUR | Jan 1 | | Attended conference at office of A.D.O.S. II A&NZA Corps. Visited Divisional Baths and Laundry. Baan noted to for 4.5 Howitzer without B.M. to replace one rendered unserviceable by premature in bore. | |
| | 2 | | Capt. R. J. BURGHAM attended conference at H.Q. NZ Calais Inf. to discuss Divisional Baths and Laundry. | |
| | 3 | | 60 Body Shields and Buchleh obtained from DADOS. 1v2 Dv to M.T.M.B. to whom they were issued. These shews to be replaced on account of consignment due from Base. | |
| | 4 | | Indents received from O.C. 5th Stf Baths for first supply of working stock of underclothing. 13 air cylinders exchanged as 2 army Heavy Mobile Workshops, Nayeloucks. | |
| | 5 | | Routine work in office. Wire for Telephone lets & equipment for W.T.M. Battery. | |
| | 6 | | Move of B/Bty 287 TB Bde to 3rd Army reported to all concerned. | |

# WAR DIARY
## or
## INTELLIGENCE SUMMARY
*(Erase heading not required.)*

Army Form C. 2118.

DADOS
or
17th Division

| Place | Date 1917 | Hour | Summary of Events and Information | Remarks and references to Appendices |
|---|---|---|---|---|
| Bar St Maur | 7 March | | Routine work. Indent for Lewis gun magazines cancelled on information received from Corps as to allotment. (4 per gun) | |
| | 8 | | Proceeded to Rontlud for purpose of purchasing stores for units. | |
| | 9 | | Noone informed of which to be cancelled owing to reorganisation of artillery. Ruthie work in Expert M.S. Parks & 17th Divisional | |
| | 10 | | Trak. Humphreys proceeded to Ordnance 2nd Army to fetch Lewis gun stocks which were subsequently handed to Q.M. 7th Loyal North Lancs. at 12.20 am on 11. III . 17 | |
| | 11. | | Capt. Bingham proceeded to Heavy Mobile Workshops 2nd Army with stores from Am Cylinder for recharging Ruthies work. 4.5 Howitzer Gun B.203 also received M gun parts for 2/7 Spare Regt. issued for | |
| | 12 | | Routine work. Arranged purchase of 150 Rag Brooms & handles. | |
| | 13. | | Parts received for Yukon ham for 150 ft. in. gun 60 | |
| | 14. | | Capt. R. J. Bingham left to report to 1st Army Headquarters G. 1st Army, anticline of munitions stores as directed by | |

WAR DIARY
or
INTELLIGENCE SUMMARY
(Erase heading not required.)

Army Form C. 2118.

DADOS 4th Division
J? Duncan

| Place | Date | Hour | Summary of Events and Information | Remarks and references to Appendices |
|---|---|---|---|---|
| Bus les ... March | 1917 15 | | Attended ADOS conference at Bailleul. Wired for one Stokes mortar to replace one burst. | |
| | 16 | | Routine work. Purchased various stores for units. | |
| | 17 | | Went to Hazebrouck to get an expedition for Stokes horns. | |
| | 18 | | Returns of linkage supplied to ADOS Corps. | |
| | 19 | | Routine work. Pte A Dalton admitted to hospital. | |
| | 20 | | Wired to Corps Salvage Officer for old clothing for Divisional School. | |
| | 21 | | Visited Railhead at Bac St Maur and Steenwerck. Routine work. | |
| | 22 | | Routine work. One Water Cart arrived for 2/4 Loyal North Lancs Regt. Wire Rope for mineral Oil for Mortars urgently required. Conference at Bailleul. | |
| | 23 | | Went for Vickers Machine Gun for 1/1st Light Trench Mortar Battery. Lewis Gun for 2/5 King's Own Royal Lancasters. | |
| | 24 | | Routine work. Wired with reference to excess demands. | |
| | 25 | | Local purchase in Bailleul. Wired for receipt of Lewis Machine Gun for 1st King's Own Royal Lancasters. | |
| | 26 | | Went to Hazebrouck to obtain an expedition for Stokes Horns. Purchased stores for 5th Div HQ. | |

**Army Form C. 2118.**

**WAR DIARY**
or
**INTELLIGENCE SUMMARY**
(Erase heading not required.)

DADOS
(?) Division

Instructions regarding War Diaries and Intelligence Summaries are contained in F.S. Regs., Part II. and the Staff Manual respectively. Title Pages will be prepared in manuscript.

| Place | Date 1917 | Hour | Summary of Events and Information | Remarks and references to Appendices |
|---|---|---|---|---|
| Dar es Salaam (?) | 28 (March?) | | Routine work. Wired for Lewis machine guns for 7th South Lancs Regt. | |
| | 29 | | Purchased stores for units at Bagilal. Routine work. Attended conference at Bagilal. Purchased stores for Stokes mortar. Purchased stores for 130th Light Trench Mortar Battery. O/c Ballon attend to duty. Routine work. Wired for Stokes Mortar. | |
| | 30 | | Lewis machine guns received for 7th South Lancs. Regt. Hastened Lewis Gun parts on race. | |
| | 31 | | Proceeded to Balcoin Base. Settled queries with O.O. Field Indents. Obtained urgent stores. Purchased Lorries for 173rd Infantry Brigade. Hastened machine gun parts. | |

31/3/17
B.H. Morgoff
Lt. Col.
DADOS
(?) Div.

D.A.G.
III rd Echelon

Herewith War Diary for month of April

1/v/17

B.J. [signature]
................................ CAPTAIN,
D.A.D.O.S. 57th WEST LANCS. DIVN.

# WAR DIARY
## INTELLIGENCE SUMMARY

Army Form C. 2118.

DADOS
57th Division
B.E.F.

Vol 3

| Place | Date 1917 | Hour | Summary of Events and Information | Remarks and references to Appendices |
|---|---|---|---|---|
| Bac St Maur | April 1st | | Routine work in office. | |
| | 2 | | Routine work in office. Obtained 300 Grenade Carriers Mustet Pattern on loan from 2nd Army troops. | |
| | 3 | | Routine work. Wired Base for Canro for steel helmets and Anti gas goggles with sponge eyepieces to replace Triplex pattern. Received 12 Lewises from 2nd Army Troops also 12 mustelet apron Bombers; Routine work. Inspection by D.O.S. cancelled. Stokes mortar received for 170th Light Trench Mortar Battery. | |
| | 4 | | Attended Conference at ADOS II Anzac (Bailleul). Purchased at various Ent 172nd Inf Brigades. Routine work in office. | |
| | 5 | | Proceeded to Bailleul to purchase Brown Shoe erring to shortage from Base. Inspected entrances for carrying Rifle him on Limbered G.S. wagons at 2/s Heavy Field Ambulance. Applied to Corps for authority to issue materials for same. | |
| | 6 | | | |
| | 7 | | | |
| | 8 | | 2 S.O. Lamps J.S. received from Base for use as area stores. Routine work. Wired for 3rd Stokes for 171st Light Trench Mortar Battery | |

Army Form C. 2118.

# WAR DIARY
or
## INTELLIGENCE SUMMARY

DADOS 57th Division

*(Erase heading not required.)*

| Place | Date | Hour | Summary of Events and Information | Remarks and references to Appendices |
|---|---|---|---|---|
| Base Camp Mons | 9 | | Visited by ADOS II Anzac. Routine work. | |
| | 10 | | Routine work. Went for Photos Mougon to enquire ne damaged Battle Quarter master. Stones of 1/5 Loyal North Lancs Regt. 2/5 Kings Liverpool Regt. 2/5, 2/8, 2/6, 2/9, 2/10 Kings Liverpool Regt. | |
| | 11 | | Proceeded to Boulud to ADOS Conference. Brought 50 Torches for 1/2 Inf — 5 Brigade. | |
| | 12 | | | |
| | 13 | | Routine work | |
| | 14 | | Visited salvage dump to arrange for return of winter clothing | |
| | 15 | | Visited salvage dumps to examine clothing. Had same all gone forward for Base. Winter clothing returned I think | |
| | 16 | | Proceeded to Army Heavy Mobile workshop for an infection | |
| | 17 | | Routine work. | |
| | 18 | | Routine work. Visited 76 King Liverpool Regt. | |
| | 19 | | Routine work. Local Puncture in Ballent | |
| | 20 | | Visited 2/5 King Liverpool Regt. Routine work | |
| | | | Interview at ADOS II Anzac land HQ Division. Routine work 5 men attached for Sgt. attendance shop. | |

DADOS
57th Division.

Army Form C. 2118.

# WAR DIARY
## or
## INTELLIGENCE SUMMARY.
(Erase heading not required.)

Instructions regarding War Diaries and Intelligence Summaries are contained in F. S. Regs., Part II. and the Staff Manual respectively. Title pages will be prepared in manuscript.

| Hour, Date, Place | Summary of Events and Information | Remarks and references to Appendices |
|---|---|---|

21st April 1917 Rue H Mann — Work for Lewis gun parts. Routine work.

22nd " — Proceeded to Estaires and Bailleul to purchase machete for cook drums and tools for Brit Showermen shop.

23rd " — Visited 2/5 Loyal N Lancs with Salvage Officer. Routine work.

24th " — Visited by A.D.O.S. T/Anger. Proceeded to Bailleul to purchase stores. Routine work.

25th " — Proceeded to Bailleul to attend Conference at Office of A.D.O.S. T/Anger. Handed over Fire Buckets to Army.

26th " — Being at Ration Farm. Routine work.

27th " — 200 extracton Jerkins gowns arrived from Base and were issued to Units. Conference at H.Q. Division.

28th " — Proceeded to T/Army Heavy Mobile Workshops at Highbrook to obtain an opinion for Showerman Irons.

(73989) W4141—463. 400,000. 9/14. H.&J.Ltd. Forms/C. 2118/10.

**WAR DIARY** *or* **INTELLIGENCE SUMMARY**

Army Form C. 2118.

DADOS

(Erase heading not required.)

Instructions regarding War Diaries and Intelligence Summaries are contained in F.S. Regs., Part II. and the Staff Manual respectively. Title pages will be prepared in manuscript.

| Hour, Date, Place | Summary of Events and Information | Remarks and references to Appendices |
|---|---|---|
| 29 April 1917 Rue du mann 30 " " | Routine work. Surrendered/transferred ch. to general. Visited by AA+QMG & DAA QMG. Proceeded to Haystonville for lunch purchases and an afternoon. Staff advised by one man returned to unit. | |

B.J.B. Lyst
30/15

D.A.D.O.S., 57th WEST LANCS. DIVN.

Secret

D.A.G.
3rd Echelon, Base.

Enclosed A.F.C. 2118, for portion of May 1917 are forwarded please.

I regret to say that these sheets were overlooked at the end of May, when balance were sent.

[Stamp: DIV. ORDNANCE OFFICER 9 JUN. 1917 WEST LANCASHIRE DIVISION, T.F.]

[Signature] Lieut.
CAPTAIN
D.A.D.O.S., 57th WEST LANCS. DIVN.

Duplicate

# WAR DIARY
## INTELLIGENCE SUMMARY
*(Erase heading not required.)*

Army Form C. 2118.

DADOS 57th Division

D.A.D.O.S., 57th WEST LANCS. DIVN.

| Hour, Date, Place | Summary of Events and Information | Remarks and references to Appendices |
|---|---|---|

B. as at Marcus
1st May 1917 — Routine work. Visited Sheng Dump.

2nd — Surveyed Rack yards, went to Lanne de Bac.

3rd — Visited by A.D.O.S. II Corps. II Corps Proceeded to Boulogne to attend conference at A.D.O.S. II Corps. Purchased amn. for Brownard foundry.

4th — Routine work. Proceeded to 2 nd Army Heavy mortars workshops Haghenwed with Pumare Range Yarigard.

5th — Routine work. Purchased esteemed kitchens for Carpenters & Saddlers.

6th — Proceeded to B_____ to purchase Soap and leather for Brownard Butter. Carpenters unless clothing to Railhead.

7th — Routine work. Enemy staked attention Bois d'Avion at 10.30 am. Successfully driven. Down Enemy announced retreat. 3.5 pm.

Appendix a

DADOS
57th Division

# WAR DIARY
## or
## INTELLIGENCE SUMMARY.
(Erase heading not required.)

Army Form C. 2118.

..................................CAPTAIN,
D.A.D.O.S., 57th WEST LANCS. DIVN.

| Hour, Date, Place | Summary of Events and Information | Remarks and references to Appendices |
|---|---|---|

8th May 1917 Pro. Lt. Maura — Wrote to Enrolpole Armo Guns and Spare parts Reg. for 1/6 Kings. Liverpool Regt. to replace in expended by the enemy.

9th — Proceeded to Th Army Heavy mobile workshops Hazebrouck to shew two cylinders for Stevens Peugeot.

10th — Attended conference at A.D.O.S. II Anzac, Bailleul. Purchased stores for special operations by 170 Inf. Brigade.

11th — Received Lewis Gun Spare Bases for 1/6 Kings Liverpool Regt. & 1/5 Bn S. Staffs Regt. Lewis Guns out of action & Spare parts wanted for.

12th — Spare parts for Lewis Guns received from Base for 1/5 Kings Liverpool Regt. brought Lewis Gun Armourer to replace one condemned exchange of 1/6 Kings Liverpool Regt.

13th — Sent further Q.F. After carriage wants for to replace two destroyed any shell fire for 175 Bty. 2nd Bde. RFA. Returned to Workshops (Hazebrouck) two Cylinders for our Cylinders pistons

Duplicate

DADOS
57th Division

Army Form C. 2118.

................ CAPTAIN
D.A.D.O.S., 57th WEST LANCS. DIVN.

# WAR DIARY
## or
## INTELLIGENCE SUMMARY.
(Erase heading not required.)

| Hour, Date, Place | Summary of Events and Information | Remarks and references to Appendices |
|---|---|---|
| 14th May 1917 Bois G. Mirror | Lieut Glew reassumed from Base for duty. Capt Lucas journeyed to Calais. Proposed started at various firms for Watch coats and other equipments to extend our equipment for Horse Ordnance Issued Return for II Army Commanders. Info received of orders by II Army Commanders, Returns wanted & unequipt with R.S.O. Demands for return of winter clothing. | |
| 16th | | |
| 17th | Attended conference at ADOS III Corps re demand of officers to retain winter clothing, the one month. Returns wrote & forwarded Demonstrating Mrs Brown. Visited ADOS IX Corps re unequipment also wanting for mounts. | |
| 18th | | |
| 19th | | |
| 20th | Investigated re Telegram 1st Army at once Went for leave, was for certainty General Supplies explain new demands for HT Lorries. | |

# WAR DIARY
## or
## INTELLIGENCE SUMMARY

Army Form C. 2118.

[Signed] Capt. J. Glenn Miller, A.D.O.S., 57th WEST LANCS DIVN

| Hour, Date, Place | Summary of Events and Information | Remarks and references to Appendices |
|---|---|---|
| 21. May 17. Bois St Maur | Visited 1st Army Gun Park and collected Emergency Ammunition Expense and Lewis gun for 1/6 Kings Liverpool Regt. Endeavoured without success to 10 Army Gun Parks for 18 pdr QF without Gun, and Carriage for C. Batty 2862 Brigade. Arrangements made to 1 Army Gun Park. | |
| 22nd | | |
| 23rd | Attended Conference at Steenje (XI Corps) re new 21 Light Mobile Workshop at Guarnerel HQ. | |
| 24th | Made arrangements with Capt. J. Penn Moulton to carry on during absence of DADOS on leave. | |
| 28. 4.17 | A.D.O.S. XI Corps made inspection of Divn wps. Collected 16 Cylinders for Stokes Mortars from OMH. Howitz. | |
| 25. 1.17 | Gun out of action 1/6 Howitzer Regt. Received loaned from Army Shops. | |
| 26. ch. | Recd. 18 Pdr Piece from 1st Army Gun Park for Cy 252 Bde. | |
| 27. th. | 18 Pdr Piece Sent to Cy 53. Brn. | |

# WAR DIARY
## or
## INTELLIGENCE SUMMARY

Army Form C. 2118.

Lieu Hulton .......... CAPTAIN,
D.A.D.O.S., 57th WEST LANCS. DIVN.

| Hour, Date, Place | Summary of Events and Information | Remarks and references to Appendices |
|---|---|---|
| 28.5.17 Bac St Naur | 2-18 Pdr Limbers recd for 285th Bn Sde R.G.A. | |
| 29.5.17 " | Recd. Stores to complete mob. frontage from Base. | |
| 31.5.17 " | Guns out of action. Parts to complete looked for | |

Army Form C. 2118.

# WAR DIARY
# or
# INTELLIGENCE SUMMARY.
(Erase heading not required.)

Vol 5

................................. CAPTAIN,
D.A.D.O.S, 57th WEST LANCS. DIVM.

| Hour, Date, Place | Summary of Events and Information | Remarks and references to Appendices |
|---|---|---|
| 1.6.17 Bac St Maur | Routine work. | |
| 2.6.1917 Bac St Maur | 1 - 3" Stokes. Returned A.S.P. 172nd T.M.B (Brigade) 2 - 2" ,, Artillery buffers x42. Thsf destined S.F. (A.B.C. IV Corps visited during) (fixed on) | |
| 3.6.17 " | Visited 1st Army M.M.M. for cylinders for Stokes Ammn. Also proceeded to 1st Army L.P. Bruay. Re urgent Sypha of T.B. cylr oil. 18Sr. P.9. Guns condemned. 1 A.A. Lt. Bty. Most Alguing (viewed & Lt Rl.) | |
| 4.6.17 | | |
| 5.6.17 | Recd 2 Guns Lot Guns from 151 Army L.P. Inspected. Proceeded to 1 Army Army Mobile workshop for 35 changed over of ensuring fred 18 L Lumphrys returned to duty, on appointed of same. | |
| 6.6.17 | One 3" Stokes T.M. + 2 - 3" T.M. received from Calais. also 18 pdr carriage from 1st Army Gun Park. | |
| 7.6.17 | Proceeded to Manville and drew G.S. Chapman Ludication 2/5 Bn. Visited by A.D.O.S XI Corps Vinted Storage | |
| 8.6.17 | Dump in afternoon. Visited HQ East Ren also "B" + Phanches | |

Army Form C. 2118.

# WAR DIARY
## or
## INTELLIGENCE SUMMARY.

(Erase heading not required.)

CAPTAIN
D.A.D.O.S., 57th WEST LANCS. DIVN.

Instructions regarding War Diaries and Intelligence Summaries are contained in F. S. Regs., Part II. and the Staff Manual respectively. Title pages will be prepared in manuscript.

| Hour, Date, Place | Summary of Events and Information | Remarks and references to Appendices |
|---|---|---|
| 9 June 1917 Bac St Maur | 13 Pdr. in charge of Aircraft Battery prematurely exploded. Gun gymetabole bent bore. 2/ 18 Pdrs. demanded on form Park to replace two withdrawn. | |
| 10 June | Brakes lost on change of 3/ 37 Battery RFA destroyed. New one demanded to replace one destroyed by shell fire in charge C Batty 586 RFA. | |
| 11 " | 18 pdr demanded to replace one destroyed by shell fire. hur one in charge C Batty 586 RFA. | |
| 12 " | Return MG gun damaged by shell fire. hur one demanded for 170.5 Machine Gun Co. | |
| 13 " | Battery in spurs reported out of action by 173rd M. Gun Co. Bearing both wired for. 13 pdr No. 1403 received for JAA Battery at Shahutine Sermen. Machine Gun received. Gun damaged for C Batty 286 RFA. Lantern internal shell hit No.4617 L.S. Howitzing withdrawn for Disposal. Pdr to replace one damaged by premature. No 437 | |
| # | 2/4 S/S + 2/5 Loyal North Lancs Regt. moved from III Canad. Divn. to 57 Div Star. | |

(73989) W4141—463. 400,000. 9/14. H.&J.Ltd. Forms/C. 2118/10.

# WAR DIARY
## or
## INTELLIGENCE SUMMARY
### D.A.D.O.S., 57th WEST LANCS. DIVN.

*(Erase heading not required.)*

Army Form C. 2118.

| Hour, Date, Place | Summary of Events and Information | Remarks and references to Appendices |
|---|---|---|
| 13 June 1917 Bac St Maur | 50th Portable Lamp Signal Lanthorn Bases to 57 K. Gun Army Lanman on 57 L Sig.t Employment G. | |
| 14 " | 2 Lewis M. Guns demanded from Gun Park for 1/6 Brigde North Lancs Regt. | |
| 15 " | One 13 pdr arrived for J. AA Battery No 1349. — meanwhile dispatched to Base. Visited by DDOS. Own accompanied by ADOS XI Corps. 2 Lewis Guns fitted by cir from Gun Park and delivered to W.L. at 5 pm. Visited H.Q. R.E. Kitchen and F. & E. Ballard. | |
| 16. | 4 st QF 18m No + 35 dispatched to Base via Steenwerk. Empties interamine returned to Base. | |
| 17. | Drew 50 Boards for Chapman Indicators from No 2 R.E. Park. Engines and delivered 45 ages to them. Purchased 42 Electric yada in Hazebrouck for 150th + 171st Inf.ry Brigades. | |
| 18. | Drew 2 Stokes 3" Mortars from XI Corps School on loan for instructional purposes. | |
| 19. | Purchased Band for R. Achilly HQ Demanded 13 pdr AA gun for J. Anti Aircraft Battery. | |

# WAR DIARY

**D.A.D.O.S. 57th WEST LANCS. DIVN.**

## INTELLIGENCE SUMMARY

*(Erase heading not required.)*

Army Form C. 2118.

| Hour, Date, Place | Summary of Events and Information | Remarks and references to Appendices |
|---|---|---|
| 20th Jan 1917 | Bde St haur Visited A.A.Q Ords at Div HQ. Routine work no office. Erected tents to accommodate extra Ammunition on extension of Gun Shops. | |
| 21st | | |
| 22nd | Visited DADOS. New Zealand Divn and O.O. II Anzac with reference to loss of equipment by 2/4 Loyal North Lancs Regt when attached from Divn. 2 Bands arrived for 4 pdr to put Lewis Guns of 1/5 Kings Liverpool Regt in action. Spares & Gauges units for Vickers MGuns and of action 1/5 South Lancs to ascertain + test ammunition for Lewis Gun out of action 1/5 Kings Liverpool Regt. 2 Bands have worked to put 1/10 Kings Liverpool Regt Lewis Guns by AA TO M/S. Routine work. Fitted Bolt heads. | |
| 23rd | | |
| 24th | Mov to Bongnies. Lewis Bun moved in to Kings Liverpool Regt. 13 pdr Anti-Aircraft gun arrived for JAA Battery. Ifpaston dispatches One Lewis Gun received for 1/3 Kings Liverpool Regt. Visited HQ Siwrange. | |
| 25th | | |
| 26th | Proceeded to I Army Gun Parks and 21 AOD. Workshop for Truck mortar parts urgently required. Parts handed over to unit | |
| 27th | 8.30 pm 4.5 QF Howitzers drawn from I Army Gun Parks and handed over to Hows Workshop. Visited + Brought from I Army Workshop | |

Army Form C. 2118.

# WAR DIARY
## of
## INTELLIGENCE SUMMARY.
D.A.D.O.S., 57th WEST LANCS.

(Erase heading not required.)

| Hour, Date, Place | Summary of Events and Information | Remarks and references to Appendices |
|---|---|---|
| 28th June 1917 Bac St Maur | Two Lephanstone Lewis Guns for B. King's Liverpool Regt received for. Guns out of action. Routine work | |
| 29th " | Four Instructive Lewis Guns issued for Practice All ranks 57th Div. | |
| 30th " | Visited Salvage Dump. Routine work | |

B.A.Moone Lt. Col.
D.A.D.O.S.
57 WLD

# WAR DIARY

## INTELLIGENCE SUMMARY

*(Erase heading not required.)*

Army Form C. 2118.

DADOS
17th Div.

| Hour, Date, Place | Summary of Events and Information | Remarks and references to Appendices |
|---|---|---|
| 1 July 1917 Bac St Maur | Visited No 21 AOD workshop (Aryies). Visited DAQMG HQ Divn. | |
| 2nd | | |
| 3rd | Visited HQ Division | |
| | Lorry despatched to Army Lorry Park to draw Carriage 4.5" How. for D Battery 78th Bde. 33 Rifles Jennings carriers also 110 sets of Pehvol in carriers. B.M. 78 pur exchange for part worn. Visited by ADOS. | |
| 4th | Inspected tools, CSt at store bases of ½ Warren Field Ambulance. Lewis Gun mirror for to replace me destroyed. 78 Kings Liverpool Regt. | |
| 5th | 7 0.17 Satur Anti aircraft (transferred to "B" A.A. Battery | |
| 6th | One Lewis gun received for ½ King Liverpolo. Visited by ADOS. and Inspector of Ammunition + Army. Lewis Gun ard of action 76 Kings Liverpool Regt. Park. Sent L.G. 75 Lgfd M.G. Lewis, Lewis gun out of action | |
| 7th | Bnt to EM. | |
| 8th | Goal bath and fetue to cravies collected from La Gorgue and Merville. | |
| 9th | When for hutch for C.R.E. Wadivis work, Lewis gun received for 1/10 Kings Liverpool Regt. | |

/ WAR DIARY
INTELLIGENCE SUMMARY.
(Erase heading not required.)

DADOS
87th Division

Army Form C. 2118.

| Hour, Date, Place | Summary of Events and Information | Remarks and references to Appendices |
|---|---|---|
| 10th July 1917 (Base St Nazaire) | Tramway crane went for 18 pdr out of action 3/8th Battery. Complete happy went for B Battery 206th Bde. Visited 18 pdr Carriage crane for B Battery 206th Bde. Visited I.O.M. No.2, A.O.D. Workshops and O.C. Corps Troops. Visits by A.D.O.S. | |
| 11th " | Routine work | |
| 12th " | Visited Sgt. M.G. Instructor | |
| 13th " | Proceeded to Base. Obtained magneto stores and hardened axletrees | |
| 14th " | Returned evening 13th | |
| 15th " | Forwarded list of units ascertained, to Havre + Rouen | |
| 16th " | 2 3" Stokes with mountings went for 171st Light T.M. Battery | |
| 17th " | Built Mr Lewis Gun 2/5 Kings Liverpool Regt. went for … | |
| 18th " | 18 pdr Carriage with Rocking Bar sights went for A 286 Bde | |
| " " | Visited by A.D.O.S. El Corps and Col. Smyth A.O.D. | |
| 19th " | Spindle Traversing went for 170th Light T.M. Battery. | |
| 20th " | Wrenches for special operations received from Gun Park for D58 Infantry Brigade Visited O "HQ Division | |
| 21st " | 1 3" Stokes went for 151st Lt T.M. Battery. | |
| 22nd " | 17.1st Aug LT.M. Battery Stokes out of action. Spindle Traversing sent for. Bricked by Aircraft. No material damage. | |

# WAR DIARY
## INTELLIGENCE SUMMARY
*(Erase heading not required.)*

Army Form C. 2118.

DADOS
57 Div

| Hour, Date, Place | Summary of Events and Information | Remarks and references to Appendices |
|---|---|---|
| 23 July 1917 Bois St Mary | Proceeded 15 cft/cm for Road Roller 170 to Infantry Brigade. | |
| 24 | Wired for 200 Blankets for Bellow in Ammunition Limbers instructional Manuals been sent to I Army. R.E. Park no openings for "A.K." mountings 16 pdr gun carriage and Rocking Bar sight for B.226 R.B. RFA sent for: shall find. Visited by ADOS XI Corps. | |
| 25 | Handed supply of 3" 3" Stokes Mortars for 171 & 172 T.M. Battery. Visited XI Corps HQ and took puncture in Bethune. One 3" Stokes T.M. wired for, for 170 Th Light T.M.B. shall find. | |
| 26 | 8 Vermorel Sprayers moved for Harland Avenue for 2 3" Stokes T.M.s. | |
| 27 | One Cart water tanks for Yorking Guard Regt moved for. 200 Gas Blankets handed Joe collected from No 16 C.C.S. Proceeded to 54 C.C.S. and collected Sight Equipment from aeroplane. | |
| 28 29 30 | | |
| 31 | Received two 3" Stokes for 170 Th Light T.M.B. and two 170 Th M.G. Co. Visited Q. Headquarters Div. Arty. Wired for (?) para for 171 Th M.G. Co. 5 DAOS 5th [?] | |

# WAR DIARY
## INTELLIGENCE SUMMARY

*(Erase heading not required.)*

**Army Form C. 2118.**

DADOS
5th Division

| Hour, Date, Place | Summary of Events and Information | Remarks and references to Appendices |
|---|---|---|
| 1st August 1917 Boes St Maur | 2" Trench Mortars condemned & 5/TMB sent one wind for. One Vickers M Gun received for 17th Wlym Bay. Routine work. | |
| 2nd " " | 200 Geo Blankets wind for 1) 1st/9th T.M. Battery. Visited mks. for 1) 2" & 3" Stokes mortars received 2) 2/Canadian TM Battery arrived. 3 Lewis guns destroyed 2/6 Kings Liverpool Regt. new gun wind for. | |
| 3rd " | Visited mks and DADOS. Routine work in office. | |
| 4th " " | 1) Muzzle Pivot mounting for Lewis guns received from 1st army R.E. Workshops XI Corps. Sent to no Ammunition Emergency Cartridge in magazines. | |
| 5th " " | 3 Lewis guns received for 2/6 Kings Royal Regt. Deferral. | |
| 6th " " | Co R.E. moved to 2nd Division. Italian supply of 100 Yukon Packs Sergt Latham proceeded to ADOS XI Corps replaced by Sgt Vincent. Visited by ADOS. | |
| 7th " " | One 3" Stokes Mortar received for 178th Light T.M. Battery. | |
| 8th " " | Visited Div. HQ. Routine work. | |
| 9th " " | Two 2" Trench Mortars (2 5/TMBattery) destroyed and new ones issued. One unserviceable M Gun 13th M Gun Co. repaired and new gun returned to 15th Army Gun Park. | |
| 10 " " | 100 Yukon Packs received from Base and receipt reported to ADOS XI Corps. Italian 2" T.M. for X 5) T.M.B. One to Mun new order. | |
| 11th " " | E.M. Carriage and R.B. Sight condemned, fire in gun pit wind for 1st/9th 3/6 Battery. | |

**WAR DIARY**

**INTELLIGENCE SUMMARY.**
*(Erase heading not required.)*

Army Form C. 2118.

DADOS
57th Division

| Hour, Date, Place | Summary of Events and Information | Remarks and references to Appendices |
|---|---|---|
| 12th August 1917, Bac St Maur | One 3" Stokes 172nd Light T.M. Battery exploded by the enemy. Bore worn for no. to replace. One 18 pdr carriage had R.B. sight condemned, shell fuse and replacement made for 426 Bde R.F.A. Wire estimate of Patrimon required to Ordnance for XI Corps. Two 2" Mortars received for 252 T.M. Battery. | |
| 13th " " " | One 2" T. Mortar received for IX 57 T.M. Battery. Visited Divl HQ. Routine work in office. | |
| 14th " " " | Hastened long outstanding returns. Visited R.A. HQ. | |
| 15th " " " | Visited by DDOS I army & ADOS XI Corps. Visited Divl HQ | |
| 16th " " " | with them. One Lewis Gun 4/5 Loyal North Lancs Regt discharged shell fire. New gun used for. Made for gear elevating and traversing for 2" T.M. | |
| 17th " " " | Reported number of ammunition in possession of M. Gun Coys to ADOS XI Corps. | |
| 18th " " " | Reported number of waterproof Return Bags required, to ADOS & Divl HQ. | |
| 19th " " " | One 3" Stokes Mortar received for 132nd Light T.M. Battery. Visited units. Routine work in office. | |
| 20th " " " | One 18pdr piece with BM. carriage & R.B. sight condemned 376 Battery, New one demanded by wire. 3" Stokes for | |
| 21st " " " | 130th Light T.M. Battery moved into place on condemned. | |

# WAR DIARY
## or
## INTELLIGENCE SUMMARY.
*(Erase heading not required.)*

Army Form C. 2118.

DADOS
J.J. ♦ Simon

| Hour, Date, Place | Summary of Events and Information | Remarks and references to Appendices |
|---|---|---|
| 22nd August 1917 Dac St Marie | No 2 Section of Reserve Parks arrived from 1st Canadian Corps. also X 60th TMB from 2nd Division. | |
| 23rd " " | Lewis gun for 4/5 Loyal North Lancs Regt. necessary. | |
| 24th " " | Wired requirements of Trumpeters to XI Corps. Local purchase at Bethune. | |
| 25th " " | 12 pdr Carriage and R.B on light underwood shell fuse 3/6 Battery no one demanded by wire. Wired to ADOS XI Corps, numbers of "Category A" men. | |
| 26th " " | Returns of blankets in Lavacuum wired to ADOS XI Corps. | |
| 27th " " | M Spence Co. moved to II Army. Wired requirements of Tarpaulins for army units to ADOS XI Corps. Visited Rifle HQ. | |
| 28th " " | Visited Depots HQ. and Salvage & myself. | |
| 29th " " | 3" Stokes mortar received for 1/o Light T.M. Battery | |
| 30th " " | Indents submitted for extra Raynor Stereoscope. | |
| 31st " " | called for Mr Cambridge Emery drill. Local purchase. | |

B.S. Morreley ht
DADOS
57 of Div

# WAR DIARY
## of
## INTELLIGENCE SUMMARY.
(Erase heading not required.)

Army Form C. 2118.

D.A.D.O.S.
57th Division

Instructions regarding War Diaries and Intelligence Summaries are contained in F.S. Regs., Part II and the Staff Manual respectively. Title pages will be prepared in manuscript.

| Hour, Date, Place | Summary of Events and Information | Remarks and references to Appendices |
|---|---|---|
| 1 Sept. 1917 Bac St Maur | Indd. Anm for Lewis Gun & Kings Liverpool Regt. indented for by one Gun not of action. | |
| 2nd " | One 3" taken unsvd for, on change 172nd F.M.B attly | |
| 3rd " | Headqrs A.A. receipt Sights for Lewis guns. Visited Brit. H.Q. | |
| 4th " | Unvd for 2 2" T.M. ober Arbr with extensions to replace damaged 2/5 T.M. Battery. | |
| 5th " | Arms kits received from Gun Park loco extension. Syl HBatteries provided to Infantries for offensive Creckit Khuth. Wrote to A.D.O.S. respecting new Armrts. Groups for 4.5 How. | |
| 6th " | matters received visit. No 1 Sect. 12 Army Corps. Stores Coy. wounded in Arm. Henderson amongst Declarations for 2" T.M Rifle for 2/5 King Liverpool Regt. T.M.S. Carry Radiator front welded for 2/9. | |
| 7th " | Visited Div. H.Q. Routine work in office. | |
| 8th " | Wrote for Bands carriers 2 Blanchero Gas Mk I. Lewis gun out of Divn. | |
| 9th " | Wrote for Lewis Traversing 18 pdr and extrador. Arm out of action & requirements of 18 pdr gun and carriages to complete units. to B.O.C. R.A. D.A.D.O.S. XI Army Corps. | |
| 10th " | Headqrs Gear elevating and Traversing for 2" M.L.T. Machine | |

DADOS
57th Division

# WAR DIARY

## INTELLIGENCE SUMMARY.

(Erase heading not required.)

Army Form C. 2118.

| Hour, Date, Place | Summary of Events and Information | Remarks and references to Appendices |
|---|---|---|
| 11th Sept 1917 Bac St Maur | Watched 18 pdr. carriage (spring) for A Battery 256/B/15 the trappelle as instrument steel find, moved No1 Section 1 Army Area. It was Bac from Ord. XI Corps Tincque to Ord. 57th Division Reserve. | |
| 12th " | 3" Stokes mortar received for 1/7th Lyft. R. Battery. Reserve Cartridge drums still from Base. All made complete. | |
| 13th " | One Lewis gun went for to replace damaged in charge 1/5 Bn Loyal N. Lancs Regt. W. Brown expending ammunition previously received. | |
| 14th " | Went for Vickers Gun for 1) 2nd Machine Gun Co. Beyond local repairs through water. | |
| 15th " | Wired all Bases to expedite reserve of Stores from 16th to 18th inst. for machine gun ammunition to another moved 5 (& A, troops & R.E. Town Major ammunition No1 Sect 1st Army Amm (trains Co. 2/3 1 TM Battery x/6 3 TM Battery, 6/332 B.battery R.3.A. 169 (3rd (MP, 376, 37), 3 H 439 Batteries also B de amm Bde. Jones mater Section HP.M. ammunition No2 Sect. Reserve Park, 1 M Transport Section, 19 & 6/38 & Sec Ammt Section Sect & No1 Grease Repairshope and 6/38th Div. Wired Base Park to expedite reserve of stores found always to increase | |
| 16th " " | moved Office and drivery to (Romins) Frontier, arms father place Bourt amm. & Stores to 35th Bn. | |
| 17th " " | 11.30 am moved Bourt Amm. & Stores to 35th Bn. Yorks R.Q.O. Lethous Local purchase in Bethune Reported move to ADOS + DDOS. | |
| 18th Nomen India. " | | |
| 19th " | Moved 1/3 1 T(M) Battery to 36th Bur. arranged supply of ammunition with QC.S) 2/Div. Notice + invited 140 1) 1/5th TM Bde | |
| 20th " | Purchased stores in Offices | |

# WAR DIARY

## INTELLIGENCE SUMMARY.

Army Form C. 2118.

DADOS 17th Division

*(Erase heading not required.)*

| Hour, Date, Place | Summary of Events and Information | Remarks and references to Appendices |
|---|---|---|
| 21st Sept 1917 Mount Forley | Visited Various units. Routine work in office. | |
| 22nd " | Delivered Show for handed units to 38th Division. Routine work in office. Visited Railhead | |
| 23rd " | Learners received for completion of Wickaratting. | |
| 24th " | | |
| 25th " | Went for one richens bomb for 172nd Machine Gun Co. To replace one lost upon transport man. One load travel used for for 7th King's Liverpool Regt. | |
| 26th " | Arranged removal of Salvage from Barry Area. | |
| 27th " | Visited units and 17th Infantry Bde HQ. | |
| 28th " | Went for 18 pdr Limber wagon and Ammunition wagon for No 2 Section DAC To replace others destroyed by shell fire, on charge of A. Rathay 2nd of Bde. Went extensive requirements of ordnance stores to R.I. Camps. Visited refilling points. | |
| 29th " | One Vickers Gun received for 172nd Machine Gun Co. Local purchase in Hazebrouck. | |
| 30th " | Visited units. Routine work in office | |

[signature] DADOS 17th Division

[signature] DADOS 17th Division

# WAR DIARY
## INTELLIGENCE SUMMARY

**DADOS**
F.J. Stinson

Army Form C. 2118.

| Hour, Date, Place | Summary of Events and Information | Remarks and references to Appendices |
|---|---|---|
| 1st October 1917 Hornet Forden | Visited units and workshops. | |
| 2nd | One 18 pdr Ammunition Wagon & one Limber Wagon received for No 2 Section DAC | |
| 3rd | Wired requirements to DOS & DDOS I Army & ADOS II Corps. Septem of 23rd Machine Gun Co DDOS I Army & ADOS II Corps proceeding to Rear. Visited 170.1 + 173 Rd Machine Gun Coys. | |
| 4th | Instrument made to return to Cetanne MC. | |
| 5th | Wires for Cartridge SAA Blank 1000 also 500 Blankets. | |
| 6th | Local purchase in Gilleno. Visited units. | |
| 7th | Wired move to all concerned (5) 34 Gm Artillery Bde. & Mortar Batteries and Heavy T Mortar Battery also Nº 150 train to Boulogne. Reported by wire to ADOS II Corps completion of issue 14 Pdr Cage Reported by wire to Brit. Artillery "TMB" of 1st Elevtrik | |
| 8th | Wired Corps LofC to stop Convoy Received instructions of annual outputs forwarded. Received 1000 Rounds SAA Blanks. Issued. Local purchase in Arres. | |
| 9th | Arranged movement of 18 Pdr Limber Wagon to Boulogne Stn. Wired all Bases to stop all issues to F.J. Stinson | |
| 10th | Reported by wire to ADOS VI Corps receipt of S. Box Respirators to replace Cert type in SWT reserve. Need 10M, 11 ⊙ 20 M. mot to continue G. partition of 18 Pdr average £27645 endorsed. | |
| 11th | | |
| 12th | Wired information re 18 Pdr average £27645 to Ordnance at Carnon & Wired Bases to transfer indent to Calais. | |
| 13th | | |

# WAR DIARY
## INTELLIGENCE SUMMARY

*(Erase heading not required.)*

Army Form C. 2118.

DADOS
57th Division

| Hour, Date, Place | Summary of Events and Information | Remarks and references to Appendices |
|---|---|---|
| 14th October 1917<br>Nonent Fosse | Reported by wire, completion of issue of issues of I.V.C. Containers Attached. ADOS XI Corps. Wrote for list of stores required by I Army Gun Park. Wrote to OO I Army Troops & OO XI Corps Troops for 200 spare steel magazines required. | |
| 15th " | Separated 4.5" How. ammunition trays to Guards Division for attachment by 57th Brit. Artillery. | |
| 16th " | Received notification of orders of artillery to 57th Division. | |
| 17th " | Wired Bury to start convoy to arrive Received 20 to next. Despatched four Lorries to Proven. Wired for 200 steel ground. | |
| 18th " Reserve Proven | Moved to Reserve. | |
| 19th " | Left Reserve for Proven. | |
| 20th " | Arranged for 160 G.S. Carts Drawn & Shrubs to provide clean thanks. | |
| 21st " | Visited B.s.s. for input stores and checked returns for revolvers etc. | |
| 22nd " | Visited XII Corps with returns to Special Stores. | |
| 23rd " | Drew special Stores from XIV Corps and delivered same to 170th Bde. | |
| 21st " Steenvoorde | Moved to Sheet 28 B.30 a 3.3. | |
| 22nd " | Visited V Army Gun Park. | |
| 26th " | Inspected Gun for Bombs. One Respirator attached. | |

**WAR DIARY**
or
INTELLIGENCE SUMMARY.
(Erase heading not required.)

Army Form C. 2118.

DADOS (-) to Division

| Hour, Date, Place | Summary of Events and Information | Remarks and references to Appendices |
|---|---|---|
| 27 Oct.17 Elverdinghe | Visited Gun Park and Salvage Dump Poperinghe. Obtained carts for limber after grenades. Wired for 4.5" How and Cart.gpl for D/58 Bde. Collected from Steam mini DADOS 3rd Division also 50 Hot Boot containers for XIV Corps. Intended by mine for 50,000 sockers. Procured Hay Bales. Wired for 4.5" How carriage for 1st How Battery 29 Bde RFA. also 100 Box Mantles also Landing carriage for 13/152 Cdn. 4. 5" Hows and carriage D/282 Bde Rose R.F.A. Limber carriage for D/152 Bde R.F.A. | |
| 28 " " | Visited 170th Bde. | |
| 30th " " | Arranged for 6 Vickers guns (for 12) Artsy Coy. delivered and taken, 9 Lewis guns for 24 L.M.L. 10 pdr carriage for cu/152 Bde R.2"kn, 12 Lewis guns for 1/5 L.M.L. 4 Lewis guns for 1/5 Kings Own Lys How & matia carriage for D/152 Bde available. Limber carriage taken for 13/152 Bde available. | |

(signature) Capt
DADOS ? Divn.

57

Army Form C. 2118.

# WAR DIARY
## or
## INTELLIGENCE SUMMARY

(Erase heading not required.)

P.A.D.O.S.
57th Division

Instructions regarding War Diaries and Intelligence Summaries are contained in F.S. Regs., Part II. and the Staff Manual respectively. Title pages will be prepared in manuscript.

| Hour, Date, Place | Summary of Events and Information | Remarks and references to Appendices |
|---|---|---|
| Blendecques 1st Apr 1917 | Went for 1 Pdr. Wagon amm[unitio]n for N° 1 Section DAC 57 Divl and 6 Lewis Guns for 1/5 Loyal N Lancs Regt. Also 1 Pdr. carriage for A/160 Bde R.F.A. | |
| 2nd " | Went for 1 Pdr. wagon amm[unitio]n for N° 2 Section 57th DAC. Indented Park to supply Books & clothing & Pack Saddlery Indented for Goats sheepskin Numnahs. | |
| 3rd " | Indented supply of Harness equipting ships | |
| 4th " | Received supply of 3 wagons G.S. N° 2 Section DAC. Went for 4.5 How. wagon limbers for D Batt[er]y L of S Bde R.F.A. 34th and 5th Divl Artillery to 34th & 26th Divisions respectively. | |
| 5th " | Cancelled indenting on Gun Park for ammn for 34 Divisionl Artillery. Went for 18Pdr limber carriage for A Batt[er]y L of S Bde also Supp'd Gun Park. Issued moved 57 Divl Artillery to Base. Moved | |
| 6th " | 1) 57 Divn. also 1) Kings Royal Regt. | |
| 7th " | moved to Zudkerque Nortch Base. | |
| 8th " | moved 34 Divl. Artl. ofonue outing in drawing indents Gun Park. Visited HQ Divn. | |
| Zudkerque 9th " | Went for 2 Vickers Guns for N° 1 Machine Gun Co. | |
| 10th " | Visited XVIII Corps. | |
| 11th " | Visited Base reference Saddles, Binoculars etc. | |
| 12th " | Went for 1 Vickers Gun for N° 3 Machine Gun Co. | |

# WAR DIARY
## INTELLIGENCE SUMMARY

Army Form C. 2118.

DADOS
57th Division

| Hour, Date, Place | Summary of Events and Information | Remarks and references to Appendices |
|---|---|---|
| Gillingham (Kent?) | | |
| 14th | Reinforcements, Rations, First Aid. | |
| 15th " | Visited Base. | |
| | Provision of No. 14 G gas masks. A gun for cemex of | |
| | Ammunition. Wired for 3' 4.5 Limbered wagons MGC RFC Pvt | |
| 16th " | Routine work. | |
| 17th " | Wired for 20 the Jachexport fighting. Indented 8 S wagons | |
| | received for 7th Flight 10th Lancer Regt. | |
| 18th | Inspected 8 Lewis hun (Enrichment) 6.0 offices XVIII | |
| | Corps Troops. | |
| 19th " | Routine work. Moved down to Squire Gatherque | |
| 20 th | Concerted indents for bombers from the for Bethune Convoy | |
| 21st | Att. Army. | |
| 22nd | Obtained Sector for transport fighting. | |
| 23rd | Routine work. | |
| 24th | Indented S.S wagons received for 1/5 the South Lanes Regt. | |
| 25th | Sun 4.5 Limbers available. Gun Park for S. 246 Pole | |
| 26th | Wired for 18 new complete units BM and carriage no 255 | |
| 27th | Pole. | |
| | 4.5 Hunt carriage available at Gun Park for D.I "/Mo | |
| 28th | 4 18 pdr limber wagons — — A Par Mo | |
| 29th | Routine work. | |

Army Form C. 2118.

# WAR DIARY
## or
## INTELLIGENCE SUMMARY

DADOS  J. L. Givens

(Erase heading not required.)

Instructions regarding War Diaries and Intelligence Summaries are contained in F.S. Regs, Part II. and the Staff Manual respectively. Title pages will be prepared in manuscript.

| Hour, Date, Place | Summary of Events and Information | Remarks and references to Appendices |
|---|---|---|
| 1) November 1917 Bethune 2nd " 3rd " 4th " 5th " 30th " | Routine work Routine work and local purchases in St Omer. Local purchases, Routine HQ Divisional & AOC. ironmongery "A" now despatched to Front (Hours) | A.J. Hinchcliffe Capt DADOS 5) A Division |

1247  W 3299  200,000  (E)  8/14  J.B.C. & A.  Forms/C. 2118/11.

Army Form C. 2118.

# WAR DIARY
## *or*
## INTELLIGENCE SUMMARY

(Erase heading not required.)

DADOS

| Hour, Date, Place | Summary of Events and Information | Remarks and references to Appendices |
|---|---|---|
| 1st Dec 1917 Jakhalpur | Returned to Bureau from Ammunition Convoy at No.14 Ord. Depot | |
| 2nd | Routine work | |
| 3rd | Ordnance handling received for 1/9 K.L.Regt & 7/10 K.L.Regt | |
| 4th | Routine work | |
| 5th | Wren Bags to stop came 6 A.T. & 6 mule vans | |
| 6th | Ord Artillery moved into line. Arrangements made to administer them. Latest news for 6 Fetter Mr Sarin | |
| | Sent stores to Panas | |
| 7th | Sent officer to Parur, Yavini Railhead | |
| 8th | Moved to Bondrugge. Ordnance undemoting. | |
| 9th Moved | Wrote suits to their stores. | |
| 10th Bondrugge | Routine work | |
| 11th | do | |
| 12th | One 18 pdr + carr. for C/255 de RFA and 2 18pdr carriages for A/86 28 6 Bde RFA available at Sun Park | |
| 13th | No.5. Further return etc now stronger and intended for issue of additional units. | |
| 14th | Wired to XIV Corps number of AA mountings for return & Lewis guns required to complete | |

Army Form C. 2118.

# WAR DIARY
## or
## INTELLIGENCE SUMMARY

(Erase heading not required.)

DADOS
SJ Brown

Instructions regarding War Diaries and Intelligence Summaries are contained in F. S. Regs., Part II. and the Staff Manual respectively. Title pages will be prepared in manuscript.

| Hour, Date, Place | Summary of Events and Information | Remarks and references to Appendices |
|---|---|---|
| 14th December 1914 recce | W[ent] for [?] [?] and mounted patrol. [?] 2/5 South Lancs Regt. [?] engaged by shell fire. Made for 2.10pm without B.M. for 18/2 B.D. New RSM not [?] [?] [?] B/500 Rds. [?] continued [?] | |
| 15th " | [?] received from Ordnance [?] [?] [?] P. 18 pdr carriages. [?] ready for [?] | |
| 16th " | Visited our dump at J. Camp also HQ. [?] artillery and Nos 11 & 12 Ordnance workshops approx running and apparent 18 pdr [?] [?] and [?] [?] NCO KA to [?] [?] on [?] No.5 Gun Park | |
| 17th " | Sent advance party and stores to J. Camp. Went the [?] 5 [?] without B. Wt + one carriage [?] D/283 18[?] RSA | |
| 18th " | J Camp. Moved office etc to J. Camp + [?] | |
| 19th " | Visited BQH HQ. Noted for 1 Victor [?] [?] + [?] | |
| 20th " | Moved for [?] return [?] [?] Jn Tr. [?] Co. [?] [?] [?] [?] new [?] [?] bought for B/260 Pol RSA | |
| 21st " | 2. yes [?] and carriages available at [?] [?] [?] D/283 B& RSA | |
| 22nd " | Running [?] [?] by AAQ my SJ Brown | |

DADOS
5th Division

**WAR DIARY**
or
**INTELLIGENCE SUMMARY**

Army Form C. 2118.

*(Erase heading not required.)*

Instructions regarding War Diaries and Intelligence Summaries are contained in F. S. Regs., Part II. and the Staff Manual respectively. Title pages will be prepared in manuscript.

| Hour, Date, Place | Summary of Events and Information | Remarks and references to Appendices |
|---|---|---|
| 24th Dec. | Routine work – Despatched Lorry to Calais to collect Cardigans & Jerseys | |
| 25 Dec. | " | |
| 26 " | Car to Calais to collect white Road enamel | |
| 27 " | " | |
| 28 " | " | |
| 29 " | " | |
| 30 " | Rec'd orders to move on 1st prox. | |
| 31 " | Handed over stores to new area. Completed move of MT stores. | |
| 1st Jan. | | |
| 2 " | | |
| 3 " | | |
| 4 " | | |
| 5 " | | |

B.L.Montgomery Capt
DADOS
5th Division

# WAR DIARY
## INTELLIGENCE SUMMARY

*(Erase heading not required.)*

Army Form C. 2118.

DADOS 57th Division

| Hour, Date, Place | Summary of Events and Information | Remarks and references to Appendices |
|---|---|---|
| Lulworth Camp Jan 1 1916 | Routine work | |
| 2 | Moved to Shorncross. Redismantled gun site on N°1 Gun Park. | |
| Shorncross 3 | Fitted up Ammunition and Armourers Shops. | |
| 4 | Work for Front corps | |
| 5 | Routine work | |
| 6 | Routine work | |
| 7 | DADOS returned from leave. Routine work. Visited Jnr 3 Supply Train | |
| 8 | DADOS returned from leave. Visited by ADOS XV Corps. Visited Bnt HQ and Bnt RA HQ. Work for Front corps. Work Jnr 8. 18 pdrs complete with carriages and supplies also 3. 6.5" Hows. complete with carriages and supplies to replace other wanted ones. | |
| 9 | Work for Visitors Mr. Gun Jr/17 it MAbs. to replace one condemned. Work for Cart water Tent for 75/Kings Lpool Regt. | |
| 10 | Visited Ordnance Gun Park N°1 and drew Supplies dealt to carrier. | |
| 11 | Routine work | |
| 12 | Visited units | |

# WAR DIARY or INTELLIGENCE SUMMARY

Army Form C. 2118.

DADOS 53rd Highland [Division]

(Erase heading not required.)

| Hour, Date, Place | Summary of Events and Information | Remarks and references to Appendices |
|---|---|---|
| Shorncliffe Jan 1914 | | |
| 13. | Captain wrote first report of DADOS from 13th Jan to 69th. | |
| 14. | Routine work. | |
| 15. | Wrote for HQrs main Sophie for Bde Bakery. | |
| 16. | Wired Corps to supply 10 auto lories & 6 hand-carts, Wired for 1/3" Stokers for 172nd I.T. Tns. Battery, which 3 off. Rect. for stores per Sophie. Arranged to draw 2000 per sophie from XI Corps Laundry. | |
| 17. | Hastened supply of leather garments. | |
| 18. | Wagon G.S. amended for 421st & 422nd Cos R.E. | |
| 19. | Wired for Vickers Mogun for 1/12th Middlx replace condemned. Arranged for issue of stores except for test washing carters. | |
| 20. | Wire for 1000 Towels for Bn. Clean Clothing Store. Attended interview at office of ADOS, II Corps, re Laundry supply of 20 Stores Sophie from Base. | |
| 21. | Local purchase in Bathlehem Steamwork. | |
| 22. | Returned special stores to test washing carters. | |
| 23. | Leather jerkins received from Base. | |
| 24. | Proceeded to OC XIX Corps Troops to select stores. | |

# WAR DIARY DADOS
## INTELLIGENCE SUMMARY 57th Division

Army Form C. 2118.

(Erase heading not required.)

| Hour, Date, Place 1918 | Summary of Events and Information | Remarks and references to Appendices |
|---|---|---|
| Steenwerck Jan 25 | Drew 1.00 p.m. General Instructions Knapton for 36th Division. Noted for 3" Stokes Gun H.Q. fitzjohn by M. Bethune | |
| 26 | Local purchases at Estaires | |
| 27 | Routine work | |
| 28 | do | |
| 29 | Hardware supply of utensils for 1914 Stars. Noted for 336th Supt. Cmpt. A Trucks for 4 instance. | |
| 30 | Routine work. | |
| 31 | Visited ADOS XV Corps. | |

A.H. [signature]
Capt.
DADOS
57th Division

Army Form C. 2118.

# WAR DIARY
## or
## INTELLIGENCE SUMMARY.
(Erase heading not required.)

DADOS 57th Division

YR/13

| Place | Date | Hour | Summary of Events and Information | Remarks and references to Appendices |
|---|---|---|---|---|
| Steenwerck | 1 | Feb | Routine work | |
| | 2 | | Eight 18 pdr with carriages for various units drawn from Ord. Gun Park No.1 | |
| | 3 | | Despatched Armourer to (1) 2nd R.De for temporary duty | |
| | 4 | | Bn't Officers Mess received for Y/L Yorkshire Regt. Cancelled units for 7/5 K. L'pool Regt & 7/3 S. Lancs Regt. (disbanded) | |
| | 5 | | 2 Vickers M. Guns received from Gun Park No.1. (rebored camera dial sight) | |
| | 6 | | Wired for Cooker Travelling body for 8th K. L'pool Regt. condemned. | |
| | 7 | | Wired for complete turnouts G.S. Wagons for Pioneer Battn. | |
| | 8 | | Rebored camera dial sight, guns out of action. (rebored dispatched units to return stores | |
| | 9 | | Settled up differences with Q Mrs of disbanded battalions | |
| | 10 | | Wired to Base for complete turnouts as they were not available in Army | |
| | 11 | | Local purchase. Visited units | |
| | 12 | | Inspected issues from 13th to 15th inclusive owing to move. | |
| | 13 | | Issued Lewis guns to R.F.A. Fd Co. R.E. + Inf Battns. for "AA" work | |
| | 14 | | Returned surplus Lewis Gun kit to Ordnance Gun Park No 1. | |

DADOS
57th Division

Army Form C. 2118.

# WAR DIARY
## INTELLIGENCE SUMMARY.
*(Erase heading not required.)*

| Place | Date | Hour | Summary of Events and Information | Remarks and references to Appendices |
|---|---|---|---|---|
| Skewsneck | 15 | 19/12 | Despatched lorry load of stores to dumps at Merville. | |
| | 16 | | Moved offices and dumps to Merville. Would Corps reference "A" news. | |
| Merville | 17 | | Visited HQ Divisions. Routine work | |
| | 18 | | "  " | |
| | 19 | | Despatched Armourers to 2/6 K.L'pool Regt & 1/2 K.L'pool Regt. for keeping duty | |
| | 20 | | Would for 100 Adjusters urgently required for drafts | |
| | 21 | | Wired for Wagon Limbers & S. for 505th Field Co. RE | |
| | 22 | | Visited Base. | |
| | 23 | | Attended Lecture on Economy by Col. Intrell AOD DOOS L of C. North | |
| | 24 | | Passed move order for A/506 Bde RFA to OOfficer 1st Army Troops | |
| | 25 | | Routine work | |
| | 26 | | 36 Pistols returned to Base 7 2nd T Mhow and mountings returned to Base | |
| | 27 | | Wires for 3rd T Motors for 170 L Sqre T. M. Battery | |
| | 28 | | Routine work. | |

A.Y Humphreys Capt
DADOS
57th Divn

Army Form C. 2118.

WAR DIARY
or
INTELLIGENCE SUMMARY.

(Erase heading not required.)

DADOS
57th Division

WB 14

| Place | Date | Hour | Summary of Events and Information | Remarks and references to Appendices |
|---|---|---|---|---|
| Marseille | 1 Feb 18 | | Verified units. | |
| | 2 | | One wagon received G.S. received for SOS Fd Bn R.E. Wheel for 18 pdr and carriage for C/285 Bde replaced unserviceable | |
| | 3 | | Wheel for 3 of above Tm for 130" F.T.M. Battery | |
| | 4 | | 18 pdr + carriage for C/285 Bde collected from Ord. hau park (A".) | |
| | 5 | | Wheel for wagon limbered G.S. two for SOS Fd bn R.E condemned | |
| | 6 | | & complete limerals for 57th Divl Signals Co | |
| | 7 | | Verified huts. | |
| | 8 | | Wired St Berges reference number of rifles with telescopic sights in possession | |
| | 9 | | Also Levies guns withdrawn from 2L (Pioneer) Bn Loyal North Lancs Regt | |
| | 10 | | Routine work | |
| | 11 | | do | |
| | 12 | | do | |
| | 13 | | Delivered stores for Austrian concentration Camps to RTO Staguille | |
| | 14 | | Routine work | |
| | 15 | | Wagon limbered G.S. received for SOS Fd Bn R.E. | |
| | 16 | | Exped receipt of discharge caps to XF Corps | |

**Army Form C. 2118.**

# WAR DIARY
## or
## INTELLIGENCE SUMMARY.
*(Erase heading not required.)*

DADOS  
XV Corps

Instructions regarding War Diaries and Intelligence Summaries are contained in F. S. Regs., Part II. and the Staff Manual respectively. Title pages will be prepared in manuscript.

| Place | Date | Hour | Summary of Events and Information | Remarks and references to Appendices |
|---|---|---|---|---|
| Meaulte | 17 | July 16 | Town shelled. Bicycles received for 5th Bn Machine Gun Corps. | |
| Le Sart | 18 | | Moved Office & dump to Le Sart. Work done to expand rooms 20 to 21st | |
| | 19 | | Sent lorry load of stores to new dump | |
| Stenhuis | 20 | | Moved to Stenhuis and took over area stores for XII Division | |
| | 21 | | Visited XV Corps. | |
| | 22 | | Routine work. | |
| | 23 | | " | |
| | 24 | | Visited new dump. | |
| La Motte | 25 | | Moved to new dump. Purchased 8 hair brushes and stones for lathes | |
| | 26 | | Collected Tarboys from RTO Etaples | |
| | 27 | | 3 sub-sheds for 6" Newton T. Mortars available at 112nd Ord. Workshops | |
| | 28 | | Routine work | |
| | 29 | | 3 "status T. Mortars received for 170 to Light T. Mortar Battery | |
| | 30 | | Suspended wires from Area | |
| | 31 | | Visited XV Corps | |

A.H. ----- Capt  
DADOS XV Corps

Army Form C. 2118.

# WAR DIARY
## or
## INTELLIGENCE SUMMARY
*(Erase heading not required.)*

DADOS.
57th Division

Instructions regarding War Diaries and Intelligence Summaries are contained in F. S. Regs., Part II. and the Staff Manual respectively. Title pages will be prepared in manuscript.

WO/75

| Hour, Date, Place | Summary of Events and Information | Remarks and references to Appendices |
|---|---|---|
| 1st April 1916 Boulogne | Visited by relieving DADOS (40th Division) | |
| 2nd " Mourelle | Moved to Mourelle | |
| 3rd " Jerbécourt | Moved to Jerbécourt was am'vie Blaton and Bermille | |
| 4th " " | Visited ADOS 5th Army. Wired for Box Respirators to Southn Base | |
| 5th " " | Moved to Boulevmer. | |
| 6th " Cantlement | Visited units of 172nd Bde. Wired for 3" Stokes for 172nd W.T.M. Battery | |
| 7th " " | Fuse sockets AOC despatched to Base 3" Stokes for 173rd F.T.M. Battery received | |
| 8th " " | Respirators made 3" Stokes for 173rd M Battery | |
| 9th " " | Moved to Beauquesne. Wired to Corps for boats. Harbord Bros. | |
| 10th " Beauquesne | Left for Ordnance Dep't Rouen to collect supplies & stores & returned | |
| 11th " " | Board grinding to units and launch Shoreham to 170 t Bde | |
| 12th " " | Moved to Jerbécourt | |
| 13th " " | " Pas-en-Artois | |
| 14th " Jerbécourt | Wires for 3 Cyl Vickers Belts Ammn on first supply for MG Battn | |
| 15th " Pas-en-Artois | Visited units | |
| 16th " " | Visited units | |
| 17th " " | 36 Lewis guns complete received for issue to Infantry Battalions | |
| 18th " " | & Lewis spt wagons G.S. received for 5 Divt Signal Co. | |
| 19th " " | Wired to Base for 50,000 ats ammunition 2 Limbers despatched to 3/10 Divn | |

Army Form C. 2118.

DADOS
57th Division

# WAR DIARY
*or*
# INTELLIGENCE SUMMARY.

(Erase heading not required.)

Instructions regarding War Diaries and Intelligence Summaries are contained in F.S. Regs., Part II. and the Staff Manual respectively. Title pages will be prepared in manuscript.

| Hour, Date, Place | Summary of Events and Information | Remarks and references to Appendices |
|---|---|---|
| 20th April 1918 Pas en Artois | Cancelled indents for 3/10 King George Regt. | |
| 21st " | Handed Base to supply on lubricating. | |
| 22nd " | Visited mill. Handed Base to supply greasing. Crew Sweeper | |
| " | amounted to No 3 C.C.S. | |
| 23rd " | Wired to Base for drain bath, 1st Royal Inniskilling Fusiliers | |
| 24 " | Visited Railhead & drawing stores fm " | |
| 25th " | Routine work | |
| 26 " | Wired to IV Corps for S.A.S Rattler Cartridges. | |
| 27 " | Asst Inspector Ammunition III Army arrived + inspected units | |
| 28 " | Wired for Lewis Guns for No 3 Section D.A.C. wanted units | |
| 29th " | Routine work | |
| 29th " | Wired for 6 Lewis guns for Trench Mortars to form supply | |
| 30 " | Visited units with Asst Inspector of Ammunition III Army. | |

B.F.K 4/6 Capt
DADOS
57 Div.

Army Form C. 2118.

DADOS
57th Division

# WAR DIARY
## or
## INTELLIGENCE SUMMARY.
(Erase heading not required.)

Instructions regarding War Diaries and Intelligence Summaries are contained in F.S. Regs., Part II and the Staff Manual respectively. Title pages will be prepared in manuscript.

WO 16

| Hour, Date, Place | Summary of Events and Information | Remarks and references to Appendices |
|---|---|---|
| 1st May Pas en Artois | Visited units | |
| 2nd " | Returned Lewis Park to supply Lewis gun lands covers. | |
| 3rd " | Wired for one Vickers gun to replace ordnance | |
| 4th " | Local purchase visited units | |
| 5th " | Wired for three 3" Stokes Mortars for (?) 2nd Light T. Mortar Batty | |
| 6th " raining | moved camp to Couin | |
| 7th " | 8 men guns received for T.s (Rs.m.s) Bn Royal N. Lancs Regt. | |
| 8th " | Received note | |
| 9th " | Wired DADOS 31st Division to pass interesting artillery records to me to 57th Div. actlty. for instructors of which for important stores | |
| 10th " | Wired for 3" Stokes mortaring for 1/21st Light T. M. Battery. Wired for 5 2" T. Mortars. (emphasises 112 may?) 1/5 Oct. Batty | |
| 11th " | Wired for Grooming bitmens R. M's 57th Div. actlty. for Nº 1 Bn. Tram. also good flour column + Bomps | |
| 12th " | Wired for 95 wagon for DA Cof. Wired for Vickers gun for N° 1 + 2 section DAC | |
| 13th " | " | A.A. figure gun for N° 1 + 2 section 3/10 |
| 14th " | Bde. W.O. out on clerk arrived from 31st Div to interview 57th Div artillery | |
| 15th " | Visited units of 57th Div. actlty. also Nº 1 & Nº 2 Tram British actlty | |
| 16th " | Wired for one Vickers gun replace ordnance shell fire. | reinpts. March 303. |

# WAR DIARY
## or
## INTELLIGENCE SUMMARY.

(Erase heading not required.)

DADOS
57th Division

Army Form C. 2118.

| Hour, Date, Place | Summary of Events and Information | Remarks and references to Appendices |
|---|---|---|
| 1 May 1918 In main | S/Cpl Marshall reported for duty. 2 L/4 pdr wagons drawn & handed over to No 3 Amm Park for A/2/5 Bde RFA. Wires to Wagon Orderlies, Hartwell Bros to supply interpreter for RA Engrs. Wires for one tripod & carriage for A/2/5 Bde RFA. | |
| 18th | Lewis gun repr to 2/5 Bn King's Own R.Lanc Regt | |
| 19th | 18 pdr & carriage returned for A/2/5 Bde R.F.A. Wires for brittle S.S wagon for 2c Kings Own R Regt. Hartwell Bros for spare canteen 303 wires for Amm limber for A/2/5 Bde RFA. | |
| 20th | Visited units. Went for 18 pdr wagon for 2 K.O.R. Fusiliers as 18 pdr Amm limbs unavail. No 3 Amm Park for 2/5 Bde Sea Rifles | |
| 22nd | Wires for 36 Lewis guns (various sorts) Purchased fodder hand. | |
| 23rd | Gas masks Routine work | |
| 24th | 36 Lewis guns received and issued unit to Gunnels. | |
| 25th | Visited 2nd Artillery units. | |
| 26th | Wires for 18 pdr unit B.M. for A/2/5 Bde RFA now available at No 3 Amm Park. Wires for various guns & tripods for 2/5 Bn 2L.F. Regt. | |
| 27th | Wires for Lewis gun complete for 2/4 Loyal N.Lanc Regt | |

Army Form C. 2118.

# WAR DIARY
## or
## INTELLIGENCE SUMMARY.

DADOS 57th Divn

(Erase heading not required.)

Instructions regarding War Diaries and Intelligence Summaries are contained in F.S. Regs., Part II. and the Staff Manual respectively. Title pages will be prepared in manuscript.

| Hour, Date, Place | Summary of Events and Information | Remarks and references to Appendices |
|---|---|---|
| 28th May 1918 Bavinel. | Went to Steual for 3rd Statin monitor for 2nd Lloyds R E Regt Lyght Tin Batty | |
| 29th " | " Lewin from 1/5 Loyal N E Regt | |
| " | At 5 P.m RFA came & took over carriage nets of 1st authent | |
| 30th " | Same and carriage went for not & available as no 3 of Park | |
| " | were for 3" Statin monitor for 171st Lyht Tm Batty | |
| 31st " | Received stores to supply wagon S.S. (Ilsen) of 1/5 KORL | |

A.T. Murphy Capt
DADOS
57th Divn

**WAR DIARY**
        **INTELLIGENCE SUMMARY.**
           *(Erase heading not required.)*

Army Form C. 2118.

DADS 857
Vol 17

| Place | Date | Hour | Summary of Events and Information | Remarks and references to Appendices |
|---|---|---|---|---|
| Lewis | June 1 | - | Received Motor Tractor for 191st L. of A. Battery | |
| | 2 | - | Started Lorries for 6" Howitzer S. Section | |
| | 3 | - | Limbered Wagon received for 2/5 K.O.R. Lancer Regt | |
| | | | " " " 1/5 Loyal N. Lancs | |
| | | | " " " 1st K.R.R. Fusiliers | |
| | 4 | - | Arrival Units | |
| | 5 | - | Wired for Rush Officers Chargers for 286 Bde R.F.A. | |
| | | | 18pr guns complete for B/286 Rde R.F.A. Condemned Fault pine | |
| | 6 | - | Wagon G.S. Lot R. 2 Lieut. B/F.A.S. | |
| | 7 | - | M.T. & Motor Kits R.A. for 2/286 Rde R.F.A. | |
| | 8 | - | Divist Travelling Limber & Coupler 9" Kings Liverpool Regt | |
| | 9 | - | Arrival Units | |
| | 10 | - | Wired for 20 Garment Aprons for 191st Infantry Bde | |
| | 11 | - | 18pr gun/carriage complete for B/285 Bde R.F.A. | |
| | | | 6" S.R. Howitzer for Y" T.M. By (N) | |
| | 12 | - | 36 Lewis guns complete for Inf. accoutrements for Inf | |

# WAR DIARY
## INTELLIGENCE SUMMARY
(Erase heading not required.)

Army Form C. 2118.

| Place | Date | Hour | Summary of Events and Information | Remarks and references to Appendices |
|---|---|---|---|---|
| Lewin | June 12 | — | Wired for 18 Pdr carriage for B/286 Bde R.F.A. | |
| | 13 | | Received 36 Lewis gun firing distributors gas. | |
| | | | Visited Units. | |
| | 15 | | Wired for 6" T.M. carrier for "X" T.M. Battery. | |
| | | | 2nd Lieut C.W. MESSER A.O.D. arrived on duty. | |
| | 16 | | Received 2-18 Pdr. Limbers for 6/286 Bde R.F.A. | |
| | 17 | | Wired for Lewis Gun parts for 26 Kings Lpool Regt. | |
| | 18 | | " Lewis Gun for 2 Bn. 57 S.A.B. | |
| | 19 | | Visited Units | |
| | 21 | | Received Stuff butter for 57 Class train. | |
| | 22 | | Visited Units & asked if all Lewis Guns were complete with spare parts. | |
| | 23 | | Wired for 18 Pdr Gun with 18 Pr. for 16/114 Bde R.F.A. | |
| | 24 | | " 3-4.5" How. with 10 Pr. for 9/186 " | |
| | 25 | | " 18 Pr. carriage with sights for 6/186 " | |
| | 26 | | Received supply of Rifles likewise for air units. | |
| | 27 | | Wired for 1 Vickers Gun for 57 Aug Bn. | |

Army Form C. 2118.

# WAR DIARY
## INTELLIGENCE SUMMARY.
*(Erase heading not required.)*

| Place | Date 1918 | Hour | Summary of Events and Information | Remarks and references to Appendices |
|---|---|---|---|---|
| Lewis | June 28 | | Hired for 6" T.M. Battel for "X" T.M. Bty. | |
| | | | - Upon Lieu G. H. for 9" King Shrop. Regt. | |
| | 29 | | Visited Units. | |
| | 30 | | Left C.W. MESSER A.O.D. took over duties as D.A.D.O.D. from | |
| | | | Major B.L. Murphy, A.O.D. | |
| | | | Attended A field and A.O.C. services for duty. | |

C. Messer
Major
D.A.D.O.D. 9th Division

30/6/18

Army Form C. 2118.

# WAR DIARY
## or
## INTELLIGENCE SUMMARY
*(Erase heading not required.)*

DADOS 57th Division

| Hour, Date, Place | Summary of Events and Information | Remarks and references to Appendices |
|---|---|---|
| Arthies 1st July 1916 | Moved from Cassel to Arthies. | |
| 2 | 39th Divisional Artillery moved to 39th Division. | |
| 3 | Wagon lines received for 39th Divisional Artillery. | |
| 4/5 | Sgt. Smith sent out and returned, despatched to 39th Division. | |
| | 10pdr with B.A. dismounted for C Battery 1st Bde replace issued, also two 3" Stokes T.M.s for 1st Se Egypt m.B. + 10pdr with B.A. for B battery 1st/5 Bde replace sent. | |
| 6 | Issued C Battery 1st Bde 1st Rde to remove 10pdr also 8 Batty 1st/5 Bde. Two guns to complete to scale "G" issued. | |
| 7 | Two 3" Stokes received for 1/70th & Lysd T.R. Btty. | |
| 8 | 18pdr carriage with eight demanded for C Batty 1st/5 Bde. Commenced general overhaul of Lewis guns. | |
| 9 | Issued C Batty 1st/5 Bde to remove 18pdr Carriage. | |
| 10 | One Vickers M Gun demanded for ambulance purpose (Army Authority) | |
| 11 | | |
| 12 } | | |
| 13 } | Nothing of importance to report. | |
| 14 } | | |
| Pan. 15 | Moved change and office to Pan-en-Artois. Demanded 10pdr with B.M. for C Batty 1st/5 Bde replace one issued. Demanded 2 sights to complete to "A" scale issued. | |
| 16 | Issued C Batty 1st/5 Bde to remove 18pdr. | |

# WAR DIARY
## or
## INTELLIGENCE SUMMARY.

**Army Form C. 2118.**

DADOS. 57th Division

| Hour, Date, Place | Summary of Events and Information | Remarks and references to Appendices |
|---|---|---|
| Rav. 17th July 1916 | Routine work. Nothing of importance to report | |
| 18 | | |
| 19 | | |
| 20 | | |
| 21 | | |
| 22 | Demanded Vickers Mtrs to replace condemned ones. Given by wire today. | |
| 23 | Lewis guns demanded to complete R.F.A. batteries to make up for losses. Major of employing repaid for duty. | |
| 24 | Lewis guns for R.F.A. Batteries received. | |
| 25 | Demanded 10 pdr for A Battery 1/2 Bde to renew 18 pdr. | |
| 26 | Wired A Battery 1/2 Bde to renew 18 pdr. Took over duties from Major Nevin. | |
| 27 | Capt. Nevin left for duty with DADOS 2nd Division | |
| 28 | Demanded 4.5" How & carriage for D/D Battery 287/1 Bde up to one brought up prisoner. | |
| Bonguinarin 29 | Moved camp & office to Bonguinarin demanded 6" T.M. & 1 YTM 13 repeat exchange | |
| Hermanville 30 | Nothing of importance to report | |
| 31 | Wired Y TMB asking to renew 6" T.M. | A.T. Humphys Major DADOS 57 th Division |

Army Form C. 2118.

# WAR DIARY
## or
## INTELLIGENCE SUMMARY.
*(Erase heading not required.)*

DADOS  
57th Division

Instructions regarding War Diaries and Intelligence Summaries are contained in F.S. Regs., Part II. and the Staff Manual respectively. Title pages will be prepared in manuscript.

| Hour, Date, Place | Summary of Events and Information | Remarks and references to Appendices |
|---|---|---|
| 1st August 1918, Hermaville | Marched over own with DA.A.G. | |
| 2nd " " | Ognigny Division moved to Ognigny Division. | |
| 3rd " " | Wired for Indian wagons & 3" Mortar ammo to Jn C/100 Bde RFA | |
| 4th " " | Vaulx under 172 Inf. Bde. | |
| 5th " " | Wired for 10 pdrs Jn C/17) Bde RFA | |
| 6th " " | I Repair available Jn C/17) Bde RFA Wired for 10pdr w carriage Jn B/303 Bde RFA available today | |
| 7th " " | Nothing to report | |
| 8th " " | Wired for 10 pdr Jn B/17) Bde RFA available | |
| 9th " " | " | |
| 10th " " | Wired for 18 pdr Jn B/17) Bde RFA available today | |
| 11th " " | Nothing to report | |
| 12th " " | Wired for 18 pdr Jn C/100 Bde RFA & 7 50 rounds for 2/100 Bde | |
| 13th " " | 10 pdr for C/100 Bde RFA available also 6 to 8 rounds for 2/100 Bde 10 pdr for B/100 available | |
| 14th " " | Wired for 3" Mortar for 12 and fused 7 hundred Battery | |
| 15th " " | " | |
| 16th " " | Nothing to report | |
| 17th " " | " | |
| 18th " " | Bombardment of enemy to be Reinforcement | |

Army Form C. 2118.

# WAR DIARY
## or
## INTELLIGENCE SUMMARY.

DADOS.
57th Division

(Erase heading not required.)

Instructions regarding War Diaries and Intelligence Summaries are contained in F.S. Regs., Part II. and the Staff Manual respectively. Title pages will be prepared in manuscript.

| Hour, Date, Place | Summary of Events and Information | Remarks and references to Appendices |
|---|---|---|
| 19 August 1918 Bouthencourt | Nothing to report | |
| 20th " | " | |
| 21st " | Indent for 6"T.M. & 4"T. Mortar Battery | |
| 22nd " | Visited units. | |
| 23rd " | Moved to Framont | |
| 24th " | Bivouacked. Moved for Mature Gun for 57th Bn M.G. Corps. Moved to Remiencourt. | 6"TM available |
| 25th " | " — " — 115 L.M.T Regt. — " — Rpdr+carriage for 18 pdr RFA. | |
| 26th " | " — " — 1/ptrs carriages for B/ 301st Bde RFA available today | |
| 27th " | Rpdr & carriage available for C/3O1stBde RFA. | |
| 28th " | Nothing to report | |
| 29th " | " | |
| 30th " | Bouy Capel Moved to Bouy Capel. Indent pair wheels for the S. Lance Regt. | |
| 31 " | Wagon ammunition moved for A/3O1 Bde RFA. | |

1/IX/18

B.S.Knight Major
DADOS
(?) Division

# WAR DIARY
## INTELLIGENCE SUMMARY

Army Form C. 2118.

DADOS 57th Division

| Hour, Date, Place | Summary of Events and Information | Remarks and references to Appendices |
|---|---|---|
| Sept 1. Bercy Capes 1916 | Wrote for 13 Pairs G.S. wheelers abt 3 18 pdr limbers + 2 carriages | |
| 2 | " " " " " " " visited DAD Vet | |
| 3 | | |
| 4 | | |
| 5 | Visited units | |
| 6 | " | |
| 7 | Wrote for 16 pdr carriages without Lyddite | |
| 8 | Visited units | |
| 9 Bernes St Marie | Visited DAC Artillery and Det HQ waggons | |
| | Bernes 172nd Bde G.S. + Det Hughes Camp RE supp. | |
| 10 | Visited units | |
| 11 | " DAC HQ | |
| 12 | Wrote to report | |
| 13 | " for 1 Vickers m. gun + 3 Lewis guns to replace loss | |
| 14 | " " 3 Lewis guns to replace loss | |
| 15 | " " " " " " | |
| 16 | Moved to Beaumont | |
| 17 Beaumont | Visited units | |
| 18 | " | |
| 19 | Wrote for 1 Webley gun | |
| 20 | " to report | |
| 21 | Visited units | |
| | | |

# WAR DIARY
## of
## INTELLIGENCE SUMMARY.

*(Erase heading not required.)*

DADOS 57th Division

Army Form C. 2118.

Instructions regarding War Diaries and Intelligence Summaries are contained in F.S. Regs., Part II. and the Staff Manual respectively. Title pages will be prepared in manuscript.

| Hour, Date, Place | Summary of Events and Information | Remarks and references to Appendices |
|---|---|---|
| Sept 23 Bavincourt | Nothing to report. | |
| 24 | Moved to Bonghen. | |
| 25 | | |
| 26 Bonghen | Visited 3rd HQ. | |
| 27 | Jothes, Johnson and Blanchets arrived from Base | |
| 28 | Wrote to & Richmond Gowap. re distribution | |
| 29 | Visited DADOS 63 (N.) Division, regarding exchange of duties | |
| 30 | Visited Divil HQ about issue of winter wear Bohair | |

W.H. Koff Major
DADOS
57th Division

Army Form C. 2118.

B.H.Q. 5/4/5 - October 1918. **WAR DIARY**
or
**INTELLIGENCE SUMMARY.**
(Erase heading not required.)

Instructions regarding War Diaries and Intelligence Summaries are contained in F.S. Regs., Part II. and the Staff Manual respectively. Title pages will be prepared in manuscript.

| Hour, Date, Place | Summary of Events and Information | Remarks and references to Appendices |
|---|---|---|
| 1st Oct 1918. | Moved Office & Dump from Boyelles to position near Bourries. Daily Routine | M.O. |
| 2nd " | Daily Routine. Demanded to replace casualties:— 21 Lewis Guns .303". 3 Vickers guns .303. 2 wagons Lim G.S. Lore 3 " " Limb 1 wagon G.S. | M.O. |
| 3rd Oct 1918 | Daily Routine. Demanded to replace casualties:— 1 wagon Lim G.S. Lore 1 " " G.S. | M.O. |
| 4th October | Daily Routine. Demanded to replace casualties:— 9 Lewis Guns | M.O. |
| 5th October | " Demanded to replace casualties:— 4 Lewis Guns wagon Lim G.S. Lore - 2 " " Limb - 3 | M.O. |
| 6th October | " Demanded to replace casualties:— 2 Lewis Guns. 2 Stokes 3" French Mortars wagon Lim G.S. Lore - 4 " " Limb 11 Major B.L. Humphreys transferred to 63rd Dn Gr Arty as D.A.A.G. Major O.D. Donnison joined S.T.A.O. " " " " from 63rd D. | M.O. |

Major S.?
R.?? ?

SA 50 57 PD - Oct 1918

Army Form C. 2118.

# WAR DIARY
## INTELLIGENCE SUMMARY.
*(Erase heading not required.)*

Instructions regarding War Diaries and Intelligence Summaries are contained in F.S. Regs., Part II. and the Staff Manual respectively. Title pages will be prepared in manuscript.

| Hour, Date, Place | Summary of Events and Information | Remarks and references to Appendices |
|---|---|---|
| Oct 7 | Daily Routine. Demanded to replace Casualties. Forded to BHQ. 10 Lewis Guns, Cart Off. Mess -1, and Iron to wagon Limp Pole -3, Cart water tank -1, Rees & Lim. Shaft -1 | |
| Oct 8 | Daily Routine &c. Demanded to replace Casualties - Lewis Guns -1, Wagon Limp Pole -4 LT Poles -1, Shaft -1 | |
| Oct 9 | Daily Routine. Tour of Units - Demanded to replace Casualties - Lewis Guns -6, Vickers Guns -4 | |
| Oct 10 | Daily Routine & Tour of Units to inspect vehicles | |
| Oct 11 | Issued 1st Winter Blanket. Loaded 2 trucks stores for reconsigning to new area. | |
| Oct 12 | Office & Dump moved to Noeux le Mines | |
| Oct 13 | Daily Routine. Demanded to replace Casualties - Wagon Lim GS Pole -1, Wagon GS -6, Shaft -1 | |
| Oct 14 | Daily Routine - Demanded to replace Casualties. Guns Lewis -1, Kitchens travelling complete -1 | |
| Oct 15 | Daily Routine - | |
| Oct 16 | Office & Dump moved to La Gorgue. Sgt S Holy rejoined S/ from 22nd Corps Mt | |
| Oct 17 | Daily Routine - Sgt Stoneman reported S/ from 22nd Corps | |

(73989) W4141-463. 400,000. 9/14. H.&J.Ltd. Forms/C. 2118/10.

# WAR DIARY or INTELLIGENCE SUMMARY

Army Form C. 2118.

DADS 5th Dn. Oct-1918

(Erase heading not required.)

| Hour, Date, Place | Summary of Events and Information | Remarks and references to Appendices |
|---|---|---|
| Oct 18th | Daily Routine & Tour of Units | MD |
| " 19th | Daily Routine & Tour of Units | MD |
| " 20th | Moved Office & Camp to Petit Ronchin (Lille) | MD |
| " 21st & 22nd | Daily Routine & Tour of Units | MD |
| " 23rd | Daily Routine. Drivers & Vets 1st new water supply arrived. Demanded to replace casualties - wagon G.S. - 1. | MD |
| " 24th | Daily Routine. Demanded to replace casualties - wagon Lim Q.F. 18pr - 1 | MD |
| " 25th | Daily Routine & Tour of Units. Demanded to replace casualties - wagon Lim Q.F. 18pr - 2, wagon Amm - 1 | MD |
| " 26th 27th 28th | Daily Routine & Tour of Units. Arranged with Supply Dept. for overhaul of M/C tyres in Armours Shop. | MD |
| " 29th | Daily Routine - Demanded to replace casualties - 2 L.T. Bodies | MD |
| " 30th & 31st | Daily Routine & Tour of Units | MD |

Major R.  
DADOS 5th Dn.

# WAR DIARY or INTELLIGENCE SUMMARY.

Army Form C. 2118.

War Diary for November 1918 — DADVS 5782

(Erase heading not required.)

Instructions regarding War Diaries and Intelligence Summaries are contained in F. S. Regs., Part II. and the Staff Manual respectively. Title pages will be prepared in manuscript.

| Place | Date | Hour | Summary of Events and Information | Remarks and references to Appendices |
|---|---|---|---|---|
| Area | 1st | | Daily Routine & Care of Units. No event of importance to record | 9822 |
| " | 2nd | | Do | |
| " | 3rd | | Do | |
| " | 4th | | Do | |
| " | 5th | | Do | |
| " | 6th | | Do | |
| " | 7th | | Do | |
| " | 8th | | Do | |
| " | 9th | | Do | |
| " | 10th | | Do | |
| " | 11th | | Do | |
| " | 12th | | Do | |
| " | 13th | | Do | |
| " | 14th | | Do | |
| " | 15th | | Do | |
| " | 16th | | Do | |
| " | 17th | | Do | |
| " | 18th | | Do | |
| " | 19th | | Do | |
| " | 20th | | Do | |
| " | 21st | | Do | |
| " | 22nd | | Do | |
| " | 23rd | | 2nd Wanted Clarke received & inured | |
| " | 24th | | Do | |
| " | 25th | | Do | |
| " | 26th | | Do | |
| " | 27th | | Do | |
| " | 28th | | Do | |
| " | 29th | | Do | |
| " | 30th | | Do | |

Memo kept by
DADVS(SM)FD.

# WAR DIARY
## or
## INTELLIGENCE SUMMARY.

Army Form C. 2118.

# WAR DIARY
## INTELLIGENCE SUMMARY.

Army Form C. 2118.

B.A.D.O.S. 57th Div.

57

| Place | Date | Hour | Summary of Events and Information | Remarks and references to Appendices |
|---|---|---|---|---|
| Lieven | 1919 Jan 8th | | Duty visits, office work, &c. United units arrived for duty | 48 |
| | 11th | 4.30 | I.B. Corps received | 24 |
| | | 12.45 | Reg. each drawn received for: 2/5 B. K.O.B. Lanc. Regt, 4/5 Bn. 9th Lanc. R'g't(?), 2/4 Bn. 9th Lanc. Regt, 2/7 K.L. Reg't, 2/4th Lancs Reg't. | |
| | 13th | | O.C. 4.5 how I workers 18th Div. received to replace others with less | |
| | | | than a quarter remaining life. | |
| | 15th | | Major P.B. Seniors left for leave to U.K. | |
| | 16th | 14.00 | Brazier received | |
| | 17th | | Visits commenced at diamond mill at Marceuil R'y to receive motilists(?) | |
| | | | equipment from units if necessary | |
| | 24th | | Visit to Boulters S.S. Sol. to ascertain quantity of Leather available | |
| | | | for purchase owing to shortage at Base | |
| | 26th | | Telegram from X Corps reporting supply of Leather to hand at Base | |
| | 27th | | Gum boots (50 pairs short, + 50 pairs (thigh)) rec'd for Div Artillery | |
| January | | | Approximately 150 units attached for administration of Ord. Services. | |

A.D.O.S. D.A.D.O.S. 57th Div.

# WAR DIARY
## or
## INTELLIGENCE SUMMARY.
*(Erase heading not required.)*

Army Form C. 2118.

DADOS 675/25

| Place | Date | Hour | Summary of Events and Information | Remarks and references to Appendices |
|---|---|---|---|---|
| | 1919. | | | |
| Juscus | 1st Feb | | Usual daily routine, nothing fresh to report. | |
| " | 2nd " | | " | |
| " | 3rd " | | " | |
| " | 4th " | | " | |
| " | 5th " | | " | |
| " | 6th " | | " | |
| " | 7th " | | " | |
| " | 8th " | | " | |
| " | 9th " | | " | |
| " | 10th " | | " | |
| " | 11th " | | " | |
| " | 12th " | | " | |
| " | 13th " | | " | |
| " | 14th " | | " | |

M Dennis
Major
DADOS 57th Division

Army Form C. 2118.

# WAR DIARY
## or
## INTELLIGENCE SUMMARY.
*(Erase heading not required.)*

Instructions regarding War Diaries and Intelligence Summaries are contained in F. S. Regs., Part II, and the Staff Manual respectively. Title pages will be prepared in manuscript.

| Place | Date | Hour | Summary of Events and Information | Remarks and references to Appendices |
|---|---|---|---|---|
| Juvours | 15 Feb | | Usual daily routine. nothing fresh to report. | |
| " | 16" " | | " | |
| " | 17" " | | " | |
| " | 18" " | | " | |
| " | 19" " | | " | |
| " | 20" " | | " | |
| " | 21" " | | " | |
| " | 22" " | | " | |
| " | 23" " | | " | |
| " | 24" " | | " | |
| " | 25" " | | " | |
| " | 26" " | | " | |
| " | 27" " | | " | |
| " | 28" " | | " | |

P. Lewis
Major
ADOS 57th Division